Alliterary
SANCOCHO

Barrel
Thanks so much
for making this a reality!
Best!

Alliterary
SANCOCHO

Marco E. Navarro

FCP

Full Court Press
Englewood Cliffs, New Jersey

First Edition

Copyright © 2013 by Marco E. Navarro

Published in the United States of America
by Full Court Press, 601 Palisade Avenue
Englewood Cliffs, NJ 07632

ISBN 978-1-938812-17-0
Library of Congress Control No. 2013941909

*Editing and Book Design by Barry Sheinkopf
for Bookshapers (www.bookshapers.com)*

Colophon by Liz Sedlack

To Dialogue

*May our chats among family, friends,
acquaintances, and strangers prove to be
as inspirational in the future
as they have been to date.*

ACKNOWLEDGMENTS

Some of the poems in this book have appeared in the following publications. I appreciate the editors' efforts in sharing my words with a larger audience:

The Acentos Review (online) : "I Read Puerto Rican Obituary," "Security Blanket"
Love's Chance Magazine: "Infatuation," "Touch"
Mad Poets Review: "Bodega"
Somos en Escrito (online): "Drifting," "Headquarterz," "Manifesto," "Veteran Way," "Position," "Time," "Birthday Blizzard"
The Haight Ashbury Literary Journal: "Quarter Hour"
The Montclair Times: "February Storm"

Published poems not included in this manuscript are:
Left Behind: "Enormity," "Quickie"

Many thanks to my immediate family: José-Manuel Navarro, Maryann B. Navarro, and Marilisa Navarro. They have been my staunch supporters through thick and thin, and continue to serve as my personal cheerleaders no matter how bad I think my draft work may be. Additional appreciation to my parents is warranted for their early and seemingly perpetual encouragement to read, expand vocabulary, analyze social and political contexts, and otherwise engage intellectually in a variety of subject matters and languages.

Thanks also to my extended family (the Navarro and

Briscoe clans), Luis Fontán, Alfredo Rojas, Laura Boss and members of her writing workshop via the Adult School of Montclair (New Jersey), Leon Walker, Deon Simmons, Erica Lewis, Hugo Reyes, Paul Cortopassi, Frank Rodríguez, Amy Williams, Marc Rubin, Cathleen Rubin, Helen Mallon, Robert Hertzberg, Luis F. Paredes, Jenielle Yasell, and Germán Castaño for their support of this work. Many of you served as my initial editors and/or reading audience. There are other friends, too many to name, that have perused my works from time to time, and/or were intrigued about my poetry writing and bigger plans. Thanks to Mauren León for the cover art, and her husband Jeff Rosenfield for assistance in brainstorming ideas and abstractions. Thanks also to Giovanni D'Amico for image sharpening and refinement. Thanks to Bookshapers and Barry Sheinkopf for this book's production.

Last, but never least, greatest thanks to a great poet and better friend, Fabián Estay, for the initial coaxing to enroll in a class together at Rutgers, The State University of New Jersey. It was originally a chance to simply chill together in an academic setting. That course was entitled "Poetry and Protest in Latin America," taught by poet Rick Kearns. That initial nudge, persuasion, and reassurance deepened my poetry interests, allowing me to grow in more ways than I could ever imagine.

—*M.E.N.*

INTRODUCTION

Why this title? I was asked this early and often, mostly from voices in my own head. I admit, in the early stages of the development of this book, from the continued writing to the selection process of what would actually be included, it was mostly mind chatter, the doubt that I would ever develop a manuscript. Then it became a personal, playful dare, to determine a way that I could captivate the mind, spark some mystery, and engage a wider readership. The primary rationale behind the title is that I wanted words that would somehow reflect aspects of my Puerto Rican and Black backgrounds, including aspects of urban living, all the while being palatable and tasty for the masses. I wanted this book to attract (hopefully) as diverse a following and readership as contained within the literary community we call poetry.

The word *sancocho* refers to a traditional soup served in various Latin American countries, including Puerto Rico. At its foundation, it typically contains pieces of meat (usually chicken or beef, sometimes both), plantain, *yuca* (known as cassava in English), and potato served in a flavored broth/stock (often beef), occasionally with peas, carrots, onions, and/or pieces of corn. Additional vegetables and starches may be included or substituted, depending on preference. Historically, *sancocho* was a dish made from scraps and leftovers. Its purpose was to provide menial sustenance for work one had completed or was about to complete. (Usually this work consisted of arduous farm or field labor.) It is, at its core, a hearty, flavorful, elegantly simple dish. It is quintessential comfort food.

Alliterary, used in the way I have devised, has a *double entendre*. I wanted to use a play of/on words. There is "alliterary," as in alliteration, or "the repitition of initial sounds in adjacent words or symbols," according to the *Merriam-Webster Dictionary*. Alliteration may be found in several pieces contained herein, although not in every piece. And then, there is the phonetic play of "a literary," or, loosely termed, "something that can be read."

Hence, the title *Alliterary Sancocho* reflects my desire to develop a scrumptious, succulent body of work that can be easily consumed, or read. Among its various spices and sprinkles of imagery, alliteration is aplenty. It is, I trust, comfort food for the spirit. It is a reminder of a larger family, a greater family, which includes you, my reader. And it is delicious.

With that, *¡buen provecho! ¡Bon appétit!* May you enjoy the taste of every word.

Table of Contents

Broths / *Caldos*

Vegetables / *Vegetales*

⌒

Meats / *Carnes*

⌒

Broths / *Caldos*

BODEGA

Humming
of refrigerator door
drowning
poignant tune of loose
spigot
drip drip dripping
goblets of water
behind cashier counter
as customer and employee
engage
in quintessential discussion of absolute
variability

Humming
overtaking soothing
voice
of earth toned beauty with
auburn hair
in spaghetti top
denim skirt
heeled sandals
seeking something
succulent
to accompany her appetite
in temporary concentration
perusing romance novels

Humming
humming seeking to be
identified
demarcated as significant
to this enterprise
as the nod recognizing presence
and the wave goodbye

Humming
unique to venue as much as
the boleros played
as background music
chirping
through ceiling speakers

INFATUATION

it hurts.
how much I like you, want to be with you, smell you.
i think I've caught feelings.

is this just passing vibe, or is it real
do you feel the same
we tend to just talk about me
with you asking questions continually.

are you afraid of expressions,
am I afraid to hear them?
will this burn out like the end of a lit match?
attracted to your beauty, ideas, intellect
i want to hold on for eternity, just hearing you speak.

every second that passes without the luscious
sound of your voice, I feel pain
longing for the sweet taste of your lips
on mine.

TOUCH

caramel skin
soft, gentle digits,
thin and slightly curved nails
enhanced at the local salon
whose polish brings forth
this delicate power and independence
in her eyes
what makes this hand so
enchanting
attractive
comforting
is its mysterious, serrated scar
in the web of the palm
between index finger and thumb

FEBRUARY STORM

snow. again. flakes gathering along nooks and
crannies of parked cars, concrete stairs, curbs, mailboxes,
and birthmarks within tree bark
demanding we take note of Mother Nature and just
slow things down, maybe change things a bit,
start anew, refresh, let our hopes run wild, and think
of new ways to connect, triggering creativity and innovation
while also pleading for us to be patient as
more wind blows, more flakes grow, forming heavier
white comforter binding us together, if only temporarily,
kindling collective imagination as we dream of
grand visions, resolving to do right in our worlds,
imagining summer's warmth and sunshine at the
Jersey shore, mouths salivating to oases of gelatos,
18" pizza slices, and funnel cakes while suspended in
rounds-merry-go, much like these words, this poem,
on this page

Birthday Blizzard

white wind white clouds
white mist
cover multicolored landscape in
white snow
fleecing busy street corners and
intersecting roadways by
resetting time with
white pause, a shush of sorts
not quite delete, almost reverse
but really just a temporary
stoppage of time
almost like God's way of telling us
to slow down, *papa*, just enjoy the view
and watch the news beyond the
immediate white window blinds
rejoice, don't do too much as
heavy winds twist between oaks,
row homes, schools, stores,
duplexes, and office buildings
reminding us that life isn't always about
the rush, but we tend to forget
we forget while we rush to
put food on the table while we
rush to pick up our kids from daycare
or karate class or piano lessons

while we rush in looking for a new job
that we feel isn't the right one
but for now, that's all we know, and
sometimes, even, in that rush it's all
we ever think we are or will be

often, the only thing that makes us
pause
is the weather, but the demanding kind
mostly in the form of a blizzard,
where nothing else can happen but
snow snow snow
where powder flakes multiply
faster than one can blink, creating
white blanket over black asphalt, gray
sidewalk, tan trash containers, and green grass,
where shrubs alive and naked due to
winter hedonism shake with exhibitionism
as two children, one boy, one girl, each in
blue jacket and black gloves, play in nearby park,
circling each other in duck-duck-goose and
hide-and-go-seek collapse momentarily to
create white snow angels while mom, in
gray pea jacket and matching hat sits
in confined crouched comfort on now-white
colored bench, internally warm from
seeing white teeth from smiles on her
bubbly brown children, reflecting on the
now, under white clouds white sky
before it gets too wet, too cold

too insane to be outside anymore
at which point it'll be time to
go home and make cozy hot chocolate with
white marshmallows

URBAN LEGEND

brisk footsteps from Adidas-covered feet
shelltoes' brilliance below frayed denim's edge
tales of a man, are they myth? is it true? is he real?
no one knows from whence he came
just that literature he narrates are his fame
unnamed character, urban pied piper,
larger than meager slender stature and with
coarse brown locks, mahogany-caramel skin
spectacled shoulder-bagged visage appears
and quickly vanishes, like a ghost, known only
as *griot* to those who dare believe

griot is magic, symbolism, analogies, and warmth
imagination perched on abandoned row house
stoop providing sunshine to badlands baddays
badmonths badyears, he brings hope to residents
endlessly shadow-covered by inner-city alleyways and
liquor-infested billboards vying for sunrays and glimmer
he is syllaballic rhythm and blues, Langston Hughes,
he is Martín Espada, Sylvia Plath, wordplay and
context intertwined with Thelonious syncopation
of Shakespeare, Parra, and Thoreau pacing restlessly on
tip of tongue, eager to reach memory's stage

griot appears at a moment's notice, paving literary

paths through patchworks of leaves and grass to
housing projects, emptied lots, or subway platforms
lobbing litanies and similes to cerebral fountains hidden
from front page news and sections metro disguised as
smiling faces under hair tousled, braided, and cornrowed
a literary Santa Claus, this man *griot*, bringing cheer to
those who seek perspective, vision, acceptance, world view

nary a casual word spoken, they say *griot* speaks truth,
voice powerful, Robeson deep, the man breathes light,
recites brilliance, acting not for an Emmy or Tony,
just a nod, a passing ear, a clap, imagining, memorizing,
improvising the grandeur of past creative visions
gifted via voice in bite-sized portions to strained brows
craving smiles, shouting the melodic erotic melancholic
to red fire hydrants, stainless steel food carts, and yellow
curbs, to streetscapes blight in dimmed sunlight and
subdued dreams

griot's got this way, this aura, this command of attention
this openness, communal generosity, this mystical spirit
morphed with confidence and determination of
an auditory postman, delivering joy, motivation,
celebration, and inspiration to eager drop boxes between
ears, two-stepping in sleepy corners, unsuspecting
street grids and subway cars, creating singular showstopper
under open top, the only act, ready to captivate and
invigorate, as eager eyes greet him tenderly like
frigid-day lips to a warm glass of cocoa, for he is
milk crate-standing thought provoker, doorstep orator,

allegoric Robin Hood, storefront muse,
barrio storyteller, eardrum superhero, this *griot*

Hemorrhage

My head bleeds clichés never-ending,
filled with negative nuances and
catchphrase conundrums as I search
to siphon silly images that do me no
good, taking my imagination for
court jester, a clown, a dunce,
for this heavy allotment of interjected
advertising and propaganda stuffs
an already crowded cranium

Crimson syrup spills from my ears,
drips from tear ducts, surfaces through
pores as would perspiration on a
humid summer evening, encasing me
in a mainstream media madness
as contagious as cholera, a cerebral
chlamydia gnawing my insatiable
hunger for revitalized expression and
scrumptious soliloquies seeking to
soothe a shaky soldier of words into
becoming a serene painter of panoramas,
yearning for a relief from the hype
for that is what is called for now, a reset
for reinvention, for refocus, over stages,
stages to wring wrong combinations

of overused phrases from thoughts,
stages to drown dozen-dimed dialogue,
stages to eliminate excess axioms

And so it bleeds, my head, offering
a cleansing, a renewal, a relief of impurities
natural or otherwise, impeding the flow
of wonderment having a reached a
tipping point within my creative core,
overloaded from the stressed opposition
of present day battling distant dreams and
desires, acting more as strangers instead
of kissing cousins

COMPARISONS

My work is exciting because it is not bland
My work is humorous because it is not straight-laced
My work is important because it is not unimportant
My work is long because it is not short
My work is beautiful because it is not ugly
My work is invigorating because it is not lifeless
My work is colorful because it is not monochromatic
My work is incomplete because it is not finished

Request

so you want to hear this poem?
one intended to conjure images of
purple rose petals, yellow tulips, of sunshine
amid shade, lush trees, and happiness.
you want to hear this poem about gentle
kisses, soft touch of palm, about
neck nuzzled noses and eye gazing
caresses, flirty flips of hair intertwined
with obvious overtures ushered as unspoken
subtle requests?
chuckling, reminded that i fell for a line, an
action that epitomizes you, just you
leading me to smile, skin tingling amid
goose bumps from passing wind.

so you want to hear this poem?
one that echoes thoughts of throwing caution
aside, inhaling assurance while mentally wading
in waters of adventure, listening to the rustling
of october leaves that soothe hesitations,
knowing that all will be okay, that my
rambling, while confusing, is explicable
that my varied interests just mean my life is
quirky, bountiful, beautiful
that my pulse, beaming from my veins,

is just active thinking, while listening to
whispering waves as we walk, talk, and
sit under the expanse of quarter moon.

so you want to hear this poem?
highway's drive with rush of vehicles
caution me to slow down and relax,
radio tunes leave subliminal clues for future
explorations, and i, lost in a dreamy fog,
write for you to hear me, hear this poem,
and its warm silence between letters.

EMPTY

I got this *reggaetón* beat just drummin' in my head
I can't let it go
like some crazy psychedelic nonsense
nagging me more than any mother would her children
with chores left undone
I'm here, kneeling, writing what seems to be garbage,
basura
trying to rid myself of all thoughts and frustrations
til I'm drained
empty
done
kaput
so that I've got nothing more to say
so that this hand gets tired scripting
so that eyes become heavy
and maybe this body levitates to my cozy bed
allowing me to dream of white sandy beaches,
of teal water, sea urchins, and playful dolphins
of curvy mermaids with curly brown hair and attractive
smiles
of a sun so comforting, its warmth tingles the skin
of tan linen trousers and white *guayaberas*
of distant island paradises

Sighs

i crave the tingling sensation of
my lover's breath massaging my forearm.

her teasing eyes coax me to
come
just   a   little   bit
closer

yeah, that's it

as we cuddle on plush green couch
feet perched on each other's laps
under blue and white comforter
watching cartoons in the
moonlit hours.

my hands caress her
right cheekbone as she
leans into my chest, exhaling
her sweet breath towards my neck.

we play with one another's fingers,
digits intermingling,
contesting, exploring, soothing
under dim flickering of

scented cinnamon candle.

she tickles me with her feet, in
socks with toes neatly fitted
like a foot's glove.

i counter with gentle squeeze of
inner thigh, causing her
surprise, bitten bottom lip, and
sensual smirk in same instance.

she snuggles even closer to this human pillow
sighing, saying nothing.

Give the Client What He Wants

So he asks a question
to make sure he understands
he receives an answer,
plainly stated
not one he likes
so he asks again, slightly
firmer
expecting something different
when all that's available as reply is
stating the obvious

LITERARY LOUNGE

Late night library is something we need
quiet place, calming space, soothing sounds
of books taken off wooden or rusted
metal shelves, pitter-patter of shoes and
sneakers along an ivory marble floor, vast
passageways among rooms inviting wind,
inspiration, and creativity to bask its rows
of cherry wood tables and matching chairs

This late night library is destined to have
reading events, speaking engagements,
maybe even a late night music hour
as the hip place to be, but not resulting
from any recent urban trend, but simply
because intelligence is sexy, debate is hot,
and expression is downright carnal sultry,
giving patrons enough reason to return
to these halls with crevices of creativity,
this archive for written words so that they
may contribute to the growing experience
of alphabetic sensuality

Heat is just enough to be cozy, cool
enough to refrain from extra garments,
smiles and surreptitious glances, chuckles

and mental telepathy, for talking is limited,
couples cozying by the main fireplace as
fathers read to lap-held daughters and sons
near the grand tree, while adolescents peruse
old jazz vinyl or rhythm and blues to get away,
regulars hide snack sneak-ins for a bite to eat
so as not to lose a favorite seat, warm book,
or research of another time

Brass desktops with green and maroon
tinted shade, vintage leather lounge chairs
with scarred, matured, and weathered skin,
grand staircases and entryways deserving
of an honored luster of this edifice
accompany wall decorations providing
snapshots in time of the surrounding
neighborhood and its residents, its
successes, its struggles and heartbeats

CARIDAD ON 33RD STREET

Peaceful, this chill time
talking to pops
obtaining insight through discussion
not lessons learned to date
understanding through listening
enjoying through breathing
articulation makes seconds pass
like express train ideas
on the line of life
individual therapy as we smell
sancocho simmering in kitchen
beneath *bachata* beat
in no rush, we eat with vigor
tasting each morsel
comida criolla delicately mingled
with Dos Equis
on our way to pursue
new avenues of exploration
and a taxi ride away
from our time for tea

ALL IS ALLEN

—borrowing from Ginsberg's essay
"All is Poetry"

Reading Ginsberg essays written between
diatribes and potent paragraphs as
extension of plethora of prose
words of bliss and truth as beautiful as
any rainbow
that contain phrases and rhythms
so wondrous, tears reach my lashes
those perfectly intermingled letters
state passion, anger, intelligence
so succinctly as Zen garden with
pebble, water droplet, and twig.

They hit me, these words on parchment
like Emeril hits his live culinary flashpan delight.
"Bam!"
It hits me in the face, shocking me, enraging me,
leaving me with whiplash and seeing stars,
yet wanting more.
All is Poetry.

Poetry is everywhere, transparent, plain as day.
Feel it testing limits through physical exertion.
Acknowledge the metronome prose of

clenching fists mandating
taut muscles and ligaments to explode
through transparent target.

It's so much more than books in ivory towers or
chats in hipster coffee shops nestled between
lattes with extra cream.
Poetry is beyond trendy hotel lobbies serving
as meeting places for freelancers with big dreams.

It's Eugene, middle-aged urban nomad
whose home is wherever his feet currently stand
armed in green knapsack serving as shield
from windy rain and surreptitious glances,
dreaming of coffee, cigarette, conversation.

Poetry is the hissing, shrieking, scraping of
archaic subway cars making next stops along
along underground pipelines.
'Tis the ding dong tune of subway car doors
and associated flutter of feet in sneakers,
Timberlands, or four inch heels.
All is Poetry, you dig?
It's ambulance sirens blaring down city streets
as oblivious, happy children play tag and kickball
in fenced playgrounds.
It's the tick tock of mounted clock drowning
the slow, pensive, silky smooth ceiling fan
lull echoing above.

Now Showing

honking horns, pumping bass, screeching brakes
passers-by searching for next sidewalk opening.
kids, 13, in baggy jeans and hoodies
articulating
nuances and social implications
of hip hop lyrics and overused sampling,
engaged in intellectual discussions as
passionate street artists pimp themselves
caricaturing tourists with
crayon on canvas
hoping to make month's rent
this time around.

scenes play like unedited independent movie
viewing backdrop with dancers of all sorts
performing for change and simple comedy
for transient Aphrodites.
voices of sidewalk marketers
peddling words and half-sentences
enticing pedestrians to enter boutiques where
everything   must   go
roasted peanuts and cashews intertwined with
mouth-watering *pinchos*
hot sauce
and pita bread

basking in front
on vendor's corner grill
near rusting parking meter and
red fire hydrant.

hypnotizing, this ordinary life. soothing.
deer-like gaze from window shopping
interrupted by
tug on right arm by friend
followed by cursing taxi man
as we make way to record shop
thinking of
Gray's Papaya
recession
specials.

FIELD WORK

Brain drain
vision impaired from
monotony
of vehicles, lights, clicks
vrooms
sun and elements with
pinch of wind,
questions, and unassuming
glances
what is he doing
as man in
orange vest
snaps shots among
intersections

TERRITORY

Oddly enough, it's funny how areas
seemingly vibrant, pleasant, and picturesque
may also lead to turf wars
among competing Good Humor
ice cream trucks

Sanctuary

I get goosebumps
my hands twitch
I nod, begin my entry routine
change clothes, wear looser-fitting
belt, say hello, stretch, and smile
think of a different time,
different place in this space
a room with cushioned floor
and red walls
with founders overlooking my
every move in prints
hung on front façade
I need just one hour

Fishbowl feeling in open room
but comfy nonetheless
a journey within at every step
aiming to focus, to reach, to achieve
and not be distracted by cacophony of
foot movements and hand gestures
of perspiration or aching joints
of snapshots and loud muddle thoughts
I listen for the sound of one hand clapping
I wait for approval of a job well done
exasperated, dehydrated, adrenaline still

rushing, I bow acknowledging my effort
I bow supporting my second family
I bow loving my raucous sanctuary
my *dojo* my safety net my 'way place'
I bow, I bow

BEATBOX

Ginsberg and Kerouac prose lead me to
improv music from human beats, pun intended,
as mind tingles and images soar like kites
sprinkling colors to the immediate blue and
expansed sky. beats and phrases from
generation past bring present to a refocused,
re-tooled, and not-so-distant recollection.
instead, quick-paced familiarity like a *déjà vu*
of sorts, done with words, intonations, sounds
from collections of letters used in rowdiness and
rapid-fire succession unveil countless treasures
of now

enlightening and serene, their words, like white ducks
fluttering in green tinged ponds as willows weep
and passers-by take daily walks in morning dew
dripping trails of breadcrumbs.
these beats, boisterous band, their words are simple,
simply enchanting the imagination providing dazzling
methodology, music to the mundane,
concise words sparkle life with such tenderness
in simplicity of detail
expressive warriors, these poets, capturing
joys of life with commonality of hardships and
distress

lyricism of their words incites me to create
my own song while i watch a loving couple, two
generations more mature, engaged in serene park
splendor as they search for untold myths in one
another's eyes as sporadic rhythmic junctions of
boom boom boom's from car speakers,
shop owners readying storefronts as the clank
clank clank of metal shades enliven, allowing
sunlight and neighborhood vibrance serve as
reminders that daily description is beat life
beatbox

Garden State Parkway

Exit 145
Ever get the itch to
dance in the aisles
of your favorite supermarket?
Give into temptation.

Exit 148
Enviable trait of humanity
is not what we plan on doing
but in simply awakening
for another day.

Exit 150
Judge a man not so much
for what he has
but rather for what he
does with what he has.

Exit 151
If music is on the mind
then be your own DJ.

BOOKSTORE CHRONICLES NO. 9

When you feel like kicking open the
door to keep from being shut out
try turning the knob first
it just might be open.

BOOKSTORE CHRONICLES NO. 42

Trust in relinquishing control
even if your first step is
letting her hold the remote.

Vegetables/ *Vegetales*

I READ PUERTO RICAN OBITUARY

(A Tribute to Pedro Pietri)

I read Puerto Rican Obituary page by page
not just the poem, more than the mere words on
parchment, but the full book
I read it because it's a rare find on the public 'shelf
located no place close except this sanctuary in
Battery Park City, hugged by other bound verses
it's out of print, deemed irrelevant, past its time
no one writes obituaries for Puerto Ricans anymore
I read it because I need stimulation after my subway
getaway, having chauffeured friends to Newark Airport
en route to a distant Motherland
I read it to ease the lactic acid of my 7 mile a.m. walk
I read it to digest my ham and scrambled morning
eggs, regular color, not green like Doctor Suess'
I read it to concoct a new metronome in my head
for a downtown Manhattan stroll, the background beat
as I go people-watching in search of vibrant corners
of unexplored minds

And it helps, you know, it helps
provide me with enough multi-orgasmic throbs
between ear ducts and heartbeats to lubricate
the slow passage of mixed fruit morsels between

esophagus and stomach
it helps test the limits of my concentration, knowing
that poetry books are never meant to be read
page by page, much less cover to cover
it helps reinforce this notion that poetry is my drug,
words are my fix, and books my dealer, with
Poets House my drug cartel nirvana
it helps to be reminded that we don't need largesse
to create artistic relevance, for beauty is innate
even under the guise of sarcasm, narcissism, bluntness,
between too much alphabetic abuse and nearly-overdosed
reality, making me a jittery mess, fiendin' for a new
prompt, another hit to get me through the next
written stanza because it's true, this Obituary, it's all
true in some way, thought-provoking, and pure,
enveloped by time, absorbing this bliss, that metaphor,
reflecting on new visions that incite yet another mental
erection, similar to one underneath board shorts, watching
beach body beauties in bathing suits being
showered with sunrays along Rockefeller and Penny Parks
perusing fashion magazines and paperback novels while
listening to tunes on iPods at a pristine urban landscape,
alien mirages to some in other sectors of Gotham City who
are just looking for a chance, another chance, a first
chance, a better chance, because in this economy, those
opportunities happen to be mutually exclusive

I read Puerto Rican Obituary page by page
and I remember
I remember stories of cold apartments with no heat

from the radiators, leaving warmed ovens open for coziness
I remember telephone booths on every other corner
at a ten cent charge, followed by rows of public phones
demanding case quarters
I remember gasoline drum fires keeping the outdoors warm,
street rubbish accessorized by flying multi-colored leaflets,
platoons of squeegee men requesting tips for unsolicited
windshield washes at red lights
I remember dope fiends, homelessness, cockroaches,
sewer rats the size of Chihuahuas and Pugs
I remember payday meaning eating *chuletas* for once this week,
while listening to Papi talk about my migrant *abuelo* picking
apples in *fincas* near Philly instead of San Lorenzo Puerto Rico

I read Puerto Rican Obituary page by page
under overhead lighting in climate-controlled conditions
allowing nary a bead of sweat to trickle from my brow
unto those tattered, donated sheets, lest I pay for a book
out of print out of circulation at a priceless cost
a memento of author activist protagonist antagonist
El Reverendo Pedro Pietri, Nuyorican cultural icon
truth preacher of all-black garb and sidewalk urban fame
I read Puerto Rican Obituary page by page
and I think of Burgos, Piñero, Perdomo, and Espada
other Boricua poets whose writings remind me of family,
of strangers I'd hope to meet, of majesty and tragedy,
comfort and strife, of a life of words filled with love even
if the journey pained the heart,
I think of this and I smile, reading with back straight, for
this text reminds me of life, not death, of our persistence

and resistance, our successes and transgressions, for
in this browned work in my even browner hands, I read
a man's love of our selves, legitimizing our worth and
experiences, if for no other reason than we continue to
survive

HEADQUARTERZ

i read, waiting in empty chair
the vacant, silver legged barber's chair
with white upholstered cushions
waiting my turn
for my time, my moment,
watching the b-movie's fight action on
flat-screen through peripheral vision
as i eagerly await the straight
edge's sharp, smooth caress of my
neck, chin, and brow
i read in this scene of cacophony
i consider comfort, a second home
this headquarterz, a sanctuary

i read among princes whose
boisterous banter is brotherhood
bravado
whose variations of brown range
from jersey city to colombia
i read among gentlemen who
rarely pick up collated
pages of text themselves,
but know lots
in fact, more than most
i read among these warriors

some of whose stories are canvassed
on palms, necks, chests, backs, or
arms like mine
through inked representations
of joys, families, histories, mantras,
hardships

i read again, for now it's my turn,
sitting in my barber's chair,
admiring DJ's subtle blend of
the temptations, brothers isley
and jay-z
i read with eyes open, spectacles off,
with 20/350 vision while
still seeing everything
i read the buzzing of hair shears
the tingling at right temple
i read the metal slip of scissors cutting
air prior to landing atop my head
i read barbers' motions of fluidity
clarity and peace,
destined to create 30 minute
masterpieces
through subtle tilts of chin
for proper coif adjustment

i read laughter meant to support
as much as joke,
empathy and encouragement
between 'cutter and client

i read the contemplation of music,
money, life, and love,
i read pride in mirrored glances
of properly shaped 'do
i read silence and intensity, knowing
poetry is in these men's deft fingertips
as much as it is in my heart

i read more at this location
of lock renovation
than i have eying books in libraries,
engaged at this moment, with
occasional entertainments of the
slow parade of wholesale mobile
butcher, dvd vendor, door-to-door
sneaker seller
i read, i read, i read
engorging myself in tales held dear
in the chests of these soldiers
whose pride manifests via
swivel of chair, isopropyl's familiar
splash behind ears, music's blasts, and
blade-to-forehead clipper
conversations

Veteran Way

i don't really think of much when
it comes to Veteran's Day i mean it
usually comes and goes nothing different
nothing special rather blasé overall but i
remember every now and then that my
grandfather my mom's dad was in World War
Two Air Force to be exact just not sure what
division or platoon or the like i just know
the result is that half my family has roots in
the Northeast the black side was here first the
Boricua side would migrate later anyway due
to his stationing in Chester Pennsylvania
we never hear him talk much about that time
as is often with things he'd rather block out
bad thoughts experiences and memories of
stuff he finds uncomfortable sometimes it
seems like it might be a secret other times like
remembering would just be too painful
similar to a living breathing nightmare

he's got all these stories my grandfather my
black american *abuelo* boy does he like to kid
a lot again not sure if it's a defense mechanism
or what but one funny story he always enjoys
telling is about the indentation he's got on

the back of his head he says that one day as
he was trying to put new shoes on a horse then
again who knew Abuelo Charles was an equestrian
after all we didn't since we lived in the city
anyway when he was putting new shoes on the
horse and wasn't looking much less paying attention
this horse bucked and kicked him right on his
doggum ass -- that was his word doggum -- and
left this big callous on the back of his black
balding head he says he didn't like to swear back
then in front of me and my sis no not in front of
the grandchildren never mind that he said ass
but let's continue

he has all these stories he is just full of them
we didn't know if they were truths or fictions
maybe somewhere in between like the time he
said he was a songwriter but only wrote one song
and it wasn't even a song more like a long stanza
and it went like this "you may mean the world
to your mother, you may mean the world to your
father, you may mean the world to your sister
and brother, too.... BUT, you're a pain in the
neck to *meeeeeeeeeeeeeeeeeeeeeeeeeeeeeeeeeeee...*"
i mean what kind of song is that much less a
stanza but we always cracked up at that one
still do in fact despite the fact that the stanza
didn't lead to any other lyrics songs or beats
let alone lines that rhymed but all i can say is
that's Abuelo Charles

my grandfather's older now approaching 100
but still thinking he's in his forties he lives in a
nursing home near the house in Philly and stays
charming and still joking it's kind of scary to realize
that he was still driving at age 90 and thinking
everything was all right while my grandmother my
Abuela Lennie his wife of sixty plus years always
was troubled when the sun began to set as she
paced back and forth to the living room windows
complaining that he wasn't home yet yeah Abuela Lennie
she died the summer of 2010 man i miss her i still
think about her anyway after a long hard troubled
joyous and fulfilling life that unfortunately she couldn't
remember much less describe it after being introduced
to Alzheimer's on a continuous basis but my grandfather
my Abuelo Charles man he's as sharp as a knife granted a
duller one now so then again maybe he's as sharp as
a spoon but still useful always joking that guy i find
it's his way of coping of dealing with the pain of a hard
life i used to get upset with him lots of these false tales
those false hopes and half-expectations i'd pray were
truly legit or of other non-committals and the like but
i don't think about that now not nearly as much anymore
i'm just happy to have him around for a bit longer
just proud to know he's lived this long enough for me
to chat and connect and get to know my Abuelo Charles

DRIFTING

I read works by great brown poets, by Pietri,
Piñero, Rodríguez, and Carlos Williams,
not knowing where ideas will take me
but I travel anyway
I write to see the landscape
beyond concrete and traffic signals
beyond honking cars and screeching tires
wait to hear serene sounds of
waves, their ebb and flow
of seagulls squawking playfully
in summer breeze on tan, sandy beaches
I sweat, perspiration trickling between
fleeting thoughts, yet instead of
angst and sadness, instead of dreams
unfulfilled and crushed realities
I think of family, I think of love
I think of Abuelo and Abuela
of palm trees and mangoes
of rice and beans, roast pork from
the pit, *pasteles* with chicken and a
teeny bit of pique, and I smile
I smile at my reflection in the
clear blue ocean water of my mind
my toes half covered in imaginary wet sand,
I dream of *piraguas*, forts, and murals

depicting an island I scarcely visit
I listen to background congas and cowbells
blend with laughter of amused children who
run to cool off in summer humidity, jump in
newly formed puddles made from opened
fire hydrants as their parents play
dominoes on old brown tray tables and
neighbors street dance to salsa, twisting
and turning to Hector Lavoe
from third floor speakers propped
on white paint-faded window sills

THANKSGIVING

sky, a tinged color, not quite orange
more reddish brown hue, hint of clouds gray
the view from car window reaching road's crest
captivates eyes as smell of burnt woodchips
and cindered leaves remind me of food
while driving to family's gratitude gathering
where aunt's homemade salsa, fried plantains,
green bananas, love, and laughter await

such occasions are events 30 strong
hugging   kissing   joking   laughing
the growing independence of my younger cousins
strengthens our family chain as young women voice
concerns of petty politics, expressing budding thoughts
as minds mature before my eyes
their joy, mitigated by minute episodes of topics'
frustrations, remains superfluously vibrant

young men acting young, acting men,
welcomed eagerly in the laps of mothers
such vistas beam as my gaze and focus shift
to my target, my second serving *entreé* of
arroz con gandules, chicken, and roast pork
accentuated by my uncle's famed codfish salad
each morsel a culinary ecstasy as my appetite

attracts discussions in awe and incredulity

the view of cascading dusk and shimmering
tree branches bring goosebumps to nape of neck
appreciating nature's autumn aromas while succulent
delights serve as palatable security blanket,
having fasted hours before in order to fully engorge
and engage the present kitchen fragrances perfuming
the air while my lips curl and nose points upward,
testing its knowledge of holiday comfort food
as succulent roasted turkey, sweet potatoes, and
pineapple-laced ham wrestle for nostril dominance

a post entrée army of peanut butter cookies,
rice pudding, and coconut candy parade themselves
for display as my choice of warm carrot cake
intermingles with cool ice cream vanilla bean and
reminds me that such times are cherished, fleeting
moments savored by containers of Tupperware

STROLL

salt-stained asphalt leads to intertwining urban
labyrinths of endless destinations and arrivals,
dreaming cityscapes pass through car windows
with storefront signs telling colorful stories like
open all night 7 days, shampoo on sale, and orange
soda buy one get one free blend with honking,
hissing, shrieking meshed with anti-lock car brake
screeching as sidewalk vent exhales, steam rising
to building tops while salt-and-pepper-haired homeless
man in blue pea coat and black Nike sneakers hovers near,
resolute in thought, encapsulating warmth within thin
blends of cotton as hurried young man with duffle
bag-draped shoulders rushes to bus on block's end
speaking aloud to no one who would listen
gotta get this gig or I don't know what I'mma do as
corporate saleswoman with Chanel handbag questions
rhetorically in Blackberry if it's all worth it while
astute Rastafari incense man says yes, baby, if it means
seeing you daily

shoes peddled on never-ending sales while shops selling
them dwindle in number, losing battles with downtown
rent and income gentrification as cursory smiles give in
to shrewd grimaces attached to tunnel vision eyes
focused forward, towards that light beyond street lamp,

the one leading to renewed hope, needed change of routine,
something different somewhere else, a place more at ease and
not as bitter, to get some perspective, invigoration, an
altering experience so this can all mean something, not just
not just inconsequential motions and sounds with glances
towards shoes and stairs and lightning-quick images with no
awareness, no patience, no peripheral, no concern
on the vision present, traveling like chattel to common
locations along varied paths among underground
arteries as subway turnstile says
-—*ding*—
you may now enter

ANNOUNCEMENT

out of breath
writhing in anguish
awaiting my division
sweat encrusting nape of neck, armpit
heartbeat bursting through debut *gi*
vein pulsing left temple
thumping and twitching cause me to
devote ignorance to right knee
my time awaits, my performance
will soon come

envisioning technique
i become obsessive compulsive
counting breathing rhythms and footsteps
from ring's edge
dicing my competition for
signs of weakness
focusing on nothing
to detect sea of patterns
becoming annoyed at anticipation
just 45 seconds
to showcase lifestyle
just 45 seconds
to demonstrate passion
just 45 seconds

and it's gone
name called
stop thinking
go

SYMPTOM

i have this thing
this thing i have
this condition, you see
is something i call
thinking too much
i think, i re-think,
i over-think, i think
some more.
and then i think about
what i think i thought,
asking others how i think
only to re-think what i
thought i think.

see, this thing
this condition i have
of thinking, rethinking,
overthinking
can get in the way of
living, just being present,
being in the moment.
i think i think about living
but i can easily think
too much about thinking,
and i wind up living less,

you know?

nevertheless, my
thoughts on thinking continue
and lead me to think,
but not so much,
yet despite thinking what
i think about how i think,
or thinking about what to
think about what i think,
you see, instead of thinking about
whatever i think i've thought,
i think now i'll just do
i'll just do.

DISCUSSION

hey, Ma, we gotta talk
I've been meaning to tell you something
there's this girl I've been seeing
yes, you met her, I've introduced you
you probably just forgot, though
Ma, you listening?
would you stop cleaning and just
listen to me, please, this is important
I'm trying to be honest with you here
and you're not making it easy
I can't stop thinking about her, Ma
damn, I can't believe I'm telling you this
stop that, you're making me nervous
it's hard enough opening up as it is
she treats me right, understands me
better than most
I'm not blushing, Ma, stop
yeah, she's slept over
she kinda lives with me too
I don't know if this is love, Ma, not sure
and why are you asking me that?
marriage? easy, Ma, it's too early
anyway that is so not an option right now
c'mon, be serious
anyway, what I wanted to tell you is

she humbles me, Ma, inspires me
huh? oh, her name?
her name is
Poetry, Ma
her name is
P
o
e
t
r
y

SERMON

We are gathered here today in this
most treasured congregation, for the
celebration, the revelation, the intonation
of the Word
But by this, I mean not the relegation
of merely a Bible, a Quran, a Torah,
or Four Vedas, no no
No, my children, I mean the Word as
our Collective Word, our collective
work, for I mean your word, my word,
her word, his word, I stand here to
preach of the Written Word, the
Listened Word, and most especially
the Spoken Word that is language
and Poetry
Can I get an "Amen?" Say, "Word."

This discussion we are having here today
is of the reverence of the Gospel
in our case the Gospel of twenty-six splendid,
uncontrolled, distinct, disheveled identities
captivating mind, body, and holy spirit
transforming our thoughts, our tongues,
our beliefs, and traditions
And this is important, Brothers and Sisters

for it is vital that we grasp, truly understand
how great the Word undoubtedly is
at the very least how it allows me to record,
to audibly document the expressions of
my visions, my empirical or researched
evidence, my criticisms, my support,
my worries, my dreams, or even my
current metaphysical state, my brethren

My proselytism would be a mere charade
without the use of the Word, of phrases,
paragraphs, and ideas, for without them,
my duty is limited – handcuffed even, for
without conversation, no connection
without alliteration, no argumentation
without interpretation, no integration
without allegation, no vibration,
may limit flow of communication
and hinder the path to literacy
Praise Word

And in this world of tall orders and omens
with you, ladies and gentlemen, as my witnesses,
I come to share a vision
A vision of a world turned up on its end
of a presence and future not seen before
A vision dramatic, dynamic, enigmatic
one so fiery, so meaningful, so simply fantastic
But let's not get ahead of ourselves, Lawd, no,
not just yet in the House of the Word

This vision, Brothers and Sisters, is of a
re-imagined landscape, not quite heaven
nor an oasis, but also no pipe dream
for it can be achieved, if believed
may be attained, if positivity maintained
for it is a stepping stone to greater senses
and sentences, causes and clauses,
but it will require work, it will demand humility
it will require faith in the Hallelujah
Can I get a "Say, 'Word'?"

I preach of a revamped sense of community
where meth-addicted child is nestled against
pin-striped vest of boardroom granddaddy
whose pride is uncompromised in public
or the workplace for the precious being
before him whom needs his nurturing

I see teen and pre-teen skaters glide and glisten
along blacktop and concrete, soaring new heights
as they listen to Beethoven and Mozart on
oft-forgotten boom boxes of yesteryear

I envision men and women dapperly dressed
with stiletto heels and Italian wingtips,
donning latex gloves and cloth surgical masks
hosting hands-on workshops of the importance
and testament that graffiti writing provides in
areas of art, creativity, and social protest

I praise the resurrection of local growth and
neighborhood rebirth through abandoned factories
transformed into art studios, flower shops,
and affordable housing, all an intimate
exploration of Urban Americana, an articulate
connection to the world in which we live
Thanks be to Word

I see these things and so may more
I call for a community that cherishes learning,
one whose creative achievements lead
not only to sustainability, but innovation,
investing in oneself for the greater good
of your neighbor and fellow beings

Let us not fear the Word, my brethren,
but embrace it, praise it, dream it, believe it
Believe in the power of the Word and its
deliverance to a more promising future
Believe in the faith of the Word and the
imagination it brings
Believe in the development of syntax
and context for a better comprehension
of life here on this bountiful Earth and
help us interact with one another
Hallelujah, Praise the Word

But the Word won't promise green pastures
No, no, ladies and gentlemen, the power of the
Word lies in the struggle to master it,

and ourselves
Through use of the Word, we may decipher
untruths of politician and preacher alike
we may form context with confidence,
chastise and critique, enlighten and encourage,
allowing us to reach a more literate life,
passionate peak, and detailed dharma

So let us give thanks to the Word,
witness its wonder, rejoice
in its ability to expand our minds,
praise the power of paragraphs,
excel in excessive eloquence,
envision our own heavens on Earth,
bask in the glory of our dreams,
and above all else,
embrace expression

In Reading's name, Amen

KARATE

empty hand
is what it's called
empty like infinite
reset, enabled
ready to do
of letting go
to learn anew, open
hand to provide force
willpower and
focus
hard and soft
tender rigidity
coarse finesse
empty hand
empty mind
never full
never stilled
open heart open sight
always flowing
begging for more
believing, achieving
regenerating spirit
as Zen thoughts
travel freely to
endless journeys and

meditations stemming from
empty grip

STARBUCKS 103

It's when you think
of nothing
that something great
sprouts forth.

Gain intuition by
trusting your gut.
Perspective is highly valued
only if it includes
more than your own.

If you want raunch, you
should be able to write raunch.
But understand the subtleties
between lust and desire.

I want to eat more than
just food. For that reason
alone, I floss daily.

Greatness comes not from
over-the-top displays.
It is most admired in
daily practices of gratitude.

ANTSY

Pent up energy yearning for
release, an outlet, to produce something
so fantastic, so profound, its notion to
confound typical thought
This energy is a wave swaying in
the ebb and flow of my veins
I sense platelets and capillaries
tingling as they move, inspiring me,
engaging me, inciting me
"Don't Stop!" "Don't sit!"
My internal beat echoes deep
in the channel of my ear canal,
seemingly more yell than mere whisper
Breathing summer's ether upon its
separation from humidity, I grow
impatient, I become edgy and agitated
as I put forth a plan to change the world,
yearning for intimately powerful thoughts
to enhance daily dialogue,
my tongue and mouth hurt from the
sting of wanting to say much more

Injured Reserve

incomplete
unbalanced
surreal purgatory
this feeling, this injury
mind wanders
psyche yearns physical activity
perspiration, tautness,
involuntary shoulder tension,
shortness of breath.
take it easy, mind says
if only it were that simple, body replies.
want to be whole again
but how soon?
soon soon
want to move like birds
tigers and iron horses again
searching for
perfection
becomes too arduous to bear on
one foot

CALL TO ACTION

I get enraged at those not prepared to open
minds as readily as mouths. I wince listening
to those who acknowledge money's good deeds,
yet ignore accolades of the exploited.
I cringe in the face of high society hangers-on
casting them aside for presence among more
endearing common folk. The time has come,
for we cannot wait for superheroes' arrival.
Words must be expressed, reality awakened.
The fleece shall be ripped from mainstream eyes.

Come explore this world with my squadron of prose.
Let us seize the day. We must defend reality as it is,
car-jack brainwashed minds, let life roam free.
See us bear fruit of untold words, fantasies of
Utopian landscapes within dilapidated downtown
centers blossoming in shape of struggle and
and counter-resistance. Cities, their struggles,
their people, their pulse are worthy of attention.

We are the lifeblood, the nervous system of society
and its symbolic landmark. Those of us who record
rhythmic beats like poets of generations past
wear that badge, hold that pen and pad with

esteem and cherished honor. This inspiration through perspiration is a gift, our juxtaposed compilation of phrases and daily diatribes are intended to inspire action based on spiritual brushstrokes on mental and vocal canvases.

We proud soldiers of poetic dialogue stand surrounded by truth-seekers and underground orators leaping to protect castles of thought deep in neglected urban labyrinths. From mere waving of our Jedi-like hands the inanimate comes alive, the stutterer becomes relaxed, the illiterate turns Rhodes Scholar, eloquent in comforting tone and soothing allegories.

The brigade of expression is here to stay. It demands to be recognized as a grassroots form, and mandates that the quintessential beauty of sunflowers blossoming among concrete jungles receive the same attention and tenderness as lilacs and tulips basking in backyards.

CASH HAIKU

Why can't money fall
from trees and clouds and grow
in backyard gardens?

Kitchen Table

Kitchen table
worn, dingy, sturdy
reverent, brown, creaky
old wood with nooks and crannies,
unanticipated curves
much like dinnertime discussions,
confessions
of smiles, jokes
laughter
swallowed in serenity of that served
favorite casserole
since steak was never an option

Kitchen table was inviting
neutral ground
discourse open, however controversial
yells, arguments,
embarrassments
never harbinger of hate
no no no, mom always said
that will never be tolerated in this house

Always good to have company
to bring forth identity
moral causes

Tuesday's evening news
young sis' new friends, however imaginary
ideas to instill as
homework gets done
since there's no desk
catching a glimpse of MTV that sis watches
dreaming of being in that next video
getting something more
something better
something beyond transition
transition
transition
it's always transition
looking at corner where
carved initials appear ancient, rooted
if only 3 months old
admiring this defacing artistry
as pops walks through door
exhausted but steadfastly
determined
to eventually spread his wings and ideas
determined
to make them stick
determined
for everyone, while trying to earn just
a wee bit more
for more opportunity,
less struggle, and
a better kitchen table

Bookstore Chronicles No. 15

Walking a mile in someone else's shoes
just leads to smelly socks
and worn soles.

BOOKSTORE CHRONICLES NO. 529

She peers eerily, subtly
not wanting to make it obvious
she plays with her curly, teased brown locks
twirling her left hand and wrist all the while
looking away while I look forward, but
ever so slowly
she has phone in her ear with
head on a swivel
canary yellow sweater, just off shoulders
with matching heels that accentuate
the curved lines of her vintage denim
she reads loose sheets, she exclaims, and
laughs aloud, head tilted back as if
to draw attention, readjusts her position
sitting back, just out of view
all the while observing
she wonders, like me, if we're really
peering to check out one another, or
merely people watching

PIANO

these hands
these hands with such lengthy, uncompromising
fingers caressing key strokes as the maestro
dabbles so effortlessly across these notes,
these melodies ringing in his head, like a long-time
imaginary friend whispering advice in one's ear,
simmering sight and sound in a
disheveled rainbow rhythm,
enveloping ears in a soft cotton quilt, sitting
fireside, enjoying the view
while the reflection of these hands,
these fingers remind us of
serene raindrops giving gentle kisses
to window panes

STILLNESS

I still want to eat sugarcane raw
as we did in Puerto Rico
basking in the sun on the patio, facing the
street
chatting with Abuelo
wiser beyond his years and
nonexistent formal education
I still want to know what his dreams are,
where he still wants to go

I still want to retrace steps and find out why
why this and why not that
these if's still cling to me, for better or worse
I still want, sometimes, to see life with
alternate endings
then again, that would make me
still want a future uncertain

I still want to be known as Poet
still want my words to reach the corporate
and the downtrodden
all in the same breath,
for both to sit at the same
intellectual dinner table, and decide to
make things better for everyone

I still want to bring my emotions to your heart,
for you to listen to my voice on paper
I still want to instill a sense of comfort
through delicious consonant and vowel gumbos

I still want to love and live lots
to gain riches more than I imagine
I still want simplistic complexity
expressive defiance and pensive serenity
I still want to think there's time

SULLEN

I wake in despair in breezy bedroom and
drained whistling of Midtown Direct
passing trains while skittish squirrels
search for platforms via brisk jumps to
tree trunks, hoping to gaze at morning
commuters whose new days bring new
promises and demands but have not yet
met last evening's responsibilities

The slow assembly line routine of shave
and shower bring familiarity in a time of
restlessness and resentment, a slow burning
candle providing glimmer of hope among
fears and day's concerns

I dress, right foot into denim pant leg, eager
for a better today but skeptical, because if
yesterday were a sign, today is forecast
to reach horse manure status, but I gallop,
mostly zombie motion, for it's been that kind
of week, that type of month in a world of
ay pobrecitos, head pats, and hugs, those
familiar empathic sayings just don't last
long enough to kick this habit, this nomadic
feeling, this lingering impermanence,
the neither here nor there, just in between

Quarter Hour

give me 15 minutes
just 15 minutes
and I'll change your mind
maybe even mine
I'll show you what we've done
write 15 words that symbolize
how glorious we are, and
how much more we have yet to do
give me 15 minutes
allow me to reset the tunes
of electric relaxation by
a tribe called quest as you
clap your hands to the song
of my de la soul and
discover new wonders
in radio wordplay
give me 15 minutes
and I'll show you 15 dreams,
innovations and surprises
share with you 15 love sonnets
15 thoughts, name you 15 colors to
create new palettes for
imaginary landscapes
allow me to share 15 stories
concocted in black cauldrons

simmering mystery and mysticism
from fairytales lush with dragons,
castles, moats, and adventure
listen as I rewrite reality
give me 15 minutes
to make you smile, laugh, love
15 minutes to make you sparkle
15 minutes to glow
to forget the ills of the world
15 minutes to cherish your company

Meats / *Carnes*

SECURITY BLANKET

Vivid memory still speaks.
Monday. MLK Day. 2006.
Parents unable to visit.
Pops got sick, typical for
this time of year.

Only it's different now.

Mom's voice quivers, uncertain,
nervous, tears held back.
Maybe you should come.
So I make plans
I go.
Call at 11:03 on train platform.
Dad's last rites given.
"I need you here. Please hurry."

Heart skips 17 beats
wondering what on Earth happened
Mind races 10,000 marathons
in three-hour trip,
seemingly timeless.
Entering emergency room
I wonder
what to do, what to say

Aunt and Mom waiting
to hug, to console,
to guide me to pops as I
I crawl on tippie-toes,
feeling 9 again.

Entering solitary room with
beeps, whistles, and bloated man
I don't recognize,
man whose vocal stature
shadows my demeanor.
Pops cannot speak,
for contraption in mouth
to keep air circulation
cuts his adjectives and activist dreams.
Father, always there to soothe me,
screams with his eyes,
leaving me helpless to hug and hold,
for doing so may cause more
internal bleeding.

So what now?

I stay.
I stay   and stay   and stay.
I get frustrated, petrified, with
quivering lips
I whimper, I scream
and stay some more.
I visit   I laugh

I sigh   I cry
and when it's time to leave
I stay again next week.
I stay for seconds
minutes hours days
and months
I stay.

I stay so much I can't remember
when I wasn't there.
Tube in throat now, still weak
and weighing 90 pounds,
Father greets me with brilliant brown eyes,
upward thumb.
I chat, I dance, I joke in ICU so much,
nurses are amazed at my levity.
No worries, Pops understands
and when he wills shoulders and head
just enough to sit upright
I nap, resting head on his lap.
He rests his hand on my forehead.

Manifesto

I don't want my poems esoteric.
I want them accessible, touchable, used in everyday
conversation. I want them to incite, evoke action with
purposeful drive even if the text is dark and sinister.
I don't want my poems naïve. No rose-colored
glasses here. Writing is hard, life is hard.
Poetry takes patience. Poetry takes effort.
Poetry takes skill and perseverance.
Every headache, every worry and fear, every crimp of
finger joints and wrist aches, every mental pace along
my antiquated, glossed, hardwood living room floor,
circling my armless leather two-seater and dingy brown
wooden coffee table, cringing over that perfect thing
to say, instead of simply writing it down.
Growing pains worth every second.

I don't want my poems sheltered and condemned
to my three-ring binder, serving as unread siblings of
imagery and random context in alphabetical order.
I want my poems visible, meaningful, published
I want the whiteness between lines of black printer ink
to gleam through like sunlight entering the bedroom from
blue curtain-draped windows shoved open, allowing surprise,
happiness and warmth to engulf an otherwise subdued existence.
I want my poems as accessible as leaflets and flyers,

bulletins and newspapers, yet handled more delicately, read
with more sincerity, than weekly junk mail circulars.

I want my poems seen as literary gifts going out of style.
I want my poems to make us laugh, cry, scream and
whistle. I want them to bewilder and excite.
I want my poems on walls, billboards, park benches,
in construction zones. I want them in bodegas, dollar stores,
upscale boutiques, and department chains.
I want them featured on Sunday morning news, sung by church
choirs, and doing rounds among talk show circuits.
I want blogs written about my poetry.
I want my poems to write their own blogs, create their own
publishing houses and chapbooks, market themselves on
street corners beside hot dog vendors and plastic drum troupes
I want them in subway stations next to keyboard players and
breakdancers, peddling words and phrases at
bargains for thought.

Manifesto Revisited

I don't want my poems esoteric.
I want them accessible, touchable, used in everyday
conversation. I want them to incite, evoke action,
move eyes, words, fears, mountains.
I don't want my poems naïve.
Allow my phrases to share the sometimes
dulled, difficult, dreary experiences that life may be
but with colorful follicle highlights.
Let readers wrestle with me over every headache, worry,
every crimp of finger joints and wrist aches,
every mental pace along my antiquated, glossed,
hardwood living room floor, circling my armless leather
two-seater and dingy brown wooden coffee table,
cringing over that perfect thing to say,
instead of simply writing it down.

I don't want my poems sheltered.
I want my poems visible, meaningful, published.
Don't want them condemned to my three-ring binder
serving as unread siblings of imagery and random
context in alphabetical order.
I want the whiteness between lines of black printer ink
to glimmer sunlight beaming from bedroom's opened
blue curtain-draped windows, allowing surprise, happiness
and warmth to engulf an unexpected artistic edification.

I want my poems voluminous like leaflets and flyers,
bulletins and newspapers, yet handled more delicately, read
with more sincerity than weekly junk mail circulars.

I don't want my poems squandered.
I want my poems seen as literary gifts going out of style.
I want them to bewilder and excite, scream and whistle.
I want my poems on walls, billboards, park benches,
in construction zones. I want them in bodegas, dollar stores,
upscale boutiques, and department chains.
I want my poems featured on Sunday morning news and
talk show circuits. I want them sung by church choirs.
I want blogs written about my poetry.
I want my poems to write their own blogs, create their own
publishing houses, market themselves on street corners
beside hot dog vendors and plastic drum troupes.
I want them in subway stations next to keyboard players and
breakdancers, peddling words and phrases at
bargains for thought.

POSITION

I want to write a political piece, but not
get all high and mighty
I want to use my words to highlight ills
of the world while brainstorming solutions
under rain clouds of hope and torrential dreams

I want to write a political piece on a grassroots
underground level, debating capitalism and
democracy as my tea server barely makes above
minimum wage and takes 3 over-the-counter meds
to offset her lack of health and insurance

I want to write a political piece about those of
us who cannot follow passions full-time
out of necessity to live day to day

I want to write about inspiring deeds of
women and men of all uniforms performing
amazing deeds here rather than be shipped
to wars in distant lands

I want to write a political piece about kids joyously
leaping upon completing 12 book compositions
and reciting excerpts from favorite essays
more readily than their excitement of

reaching the next round on that video game
du mode on PS3 or Xbox

I want to write about folks in 'hoods and barrios
investing in on-line and off-line bank accounts
instead of sneaker pair #8 for the quarter

I want to write a political piece of putting forth
endowments in mental neighborhood growth
and less in 22-inch rims, of cleaning garbage off
streets and hosting chess tournaments in dark
alleys, of engaging in discussion so mind-boggling
its only comparison is multi-orgasmic sex

I want to write a political piece
I want to write a political
I want to write a politic
I want to write a polit
I just want to write

TIME

is what this is about
it's about time that this all makes sense
it's about figuring out what exactly is
going on, and working from there
it's about getting past the indecisive
phase and moving forward
it's about letting go and thinking of the best
as baby steps turn to noticeable strides
it's about growing strong but not
growing up
it's about leaving nervousness and
anxiety at the doorstep to be thrown out
with recyclables and other trash today
because they're not wanted indoors
it's about maintaining friendships and
developing new ones
it's about patience for patience alone
it's about knowing, really knowing, that
you're here for a purpose, and not just
going for it, but living it, because it's the best
thing for you, and as a result, for us
because your best my best her best is best
in fact it's our most valued asset
it's about seeing love and going for broke
as if there's no tomorrow

pursuing your dharma even if your path
is temporarily road blocked
it's about not knowing, yet continuing
because eventually it will come
and in doing so, in keeping the ball rolling,
gaining momentum or inspiration
maybe these lines eventually carry deeper
truth and meaning than originally anticipated
and in the end, when that time arrives, it
makes this time more meaningful, for
that's about all it ever was, all
it's ever been

Lip Service

Your notions of revolutions are unsound and untrue.
Come close. Pay attention. Allow me to educate you.

Lip service, young stranger, does not a revolution make.
It ain't a walk in the park, 'tis not a piece of cake.
You ain't ready, kid, your mission has no substance.
You don't know what it means to stand against injustice.
Ya bought into false notions and white man enmity.
This ain't about talkin' slick, or quotin' Public Enemy.

You believe in anarchy and chaos as the form of ends and means
but have no idea how to bridge this reality with true dreams.
Masturbatin' at pumped fists, Afro picks, and picket sign
but when it comes to moral causes you keep quiet, as if all is fine.
These aren't things to shrug off as merely 'just because's
you disgrace those to whom you owe multiple applauses.

Can't believe you're so naïve to use dumb, metaphorical clichés.
Revolution means more to me than stickers in window displays.
You say you want a revolution? That's bull. I'm calling you out.
Yo, for real, please stop whinin' – ain't no need to pout.
Revolution? Are you serious? You don't know meaning o' the word.
Did I stutter, motherfucker? Yes, I said just what you heard.

Revolution is Rosa's "no," Malcolm's X, Ali's goodbye to Clay.

It's also small resistance to unjust actions day-to-day.
Revolution is Zapata, Neruda, Chomsky, Grito de Lares.
It's Julia de Burgos, Albizu, Hostos, and even Rubén Blades.

Revolution is a spiritual awakenin', denomination irrespective.
Might be reachin' personal goals, or aspirations for the collective.
It's marchin', believin', achievement, and so much more
but too many o' y'all think realness must be just either/or.
But why? Why? Understand this here, see,
revolution is about the word "and," intertwined with authenticity.
Like attorney and street artist, public defender and foster mother,
janitor, doorman, chef, teacher, and big brother.
Shoot, for all I know it's poet and engineer.
Still listenin', *mi gente*? Just tryin' to make things clear.

Revolution is passion, intensity, by all means necessary
attainin' our ultimate dreams, making us legendary.
It's stripper with three kids, strivin', doin' what she may
to achieve a better future by obtainin' an MBA.
It's the college student with free schooling makin' money in higher ed,
with schol'rship check in purse, applied science in her head.
It's homeless man on the corner requestin' meager change
to buy texts from Strand Bookstore, increasin' intellectual range.

Revolution is reality, and makin' it much better.
It ain't about being smooth, ain't about being clever.
It may be losin' a job for now but still winnin' the game of life,
it's pushin' forward when it's hardest while acknowledgin' the strife.
It's understandin' limitations and askin' for a hand
knowin' there's a higher purpose for us all on this lush, expansive land.

Revolution is freedom for him, her, me, and you.
It's purposeful tenacity, dawg, the act of followin' through.

So while you're sitting here all cute, you fake ass wannabe,
in your pretty jeans, hemp shoulder bag, and red Che-faced fitted T,
listen real closely, son, this is important to me.
It's not a hobby, not 'bout a brand, but developin' a legacy.
Razor vision focus merged with flexibility
that is real, that is progress, that true revolution be.
So with these thoughts, I leave you my main conclusion:
Revolution, comprehend, is the evolution of resolution.

BOOKSTORE CHRONICLES NO. 78

1.
Rudimentary activities
allow me to engage in
Zen practice

2.
I write because I can
I read because I write
I am because I read

DÉJÀ VU

My father, Dr. José-Manuel Navarro,
historian, educator, influencer, first-born
lies awake in Penn Hospital's intensive care
shaken, weak, frustrated, yet very much alive
knowledgeable of his near-death condition in
two languages, English and Spanish,
survivor of mitral-valve bacterial infection,
forty-pound weight loss, and endocarditis,
eagerly awaits his release on a day not today.

Across the hall in the far room next to corner
Doña Lucía, wife of migrant worker
Ernesto Fulano de Tal, is also gravely ill
seriousness of terms explained in medical English
not understood by most family members,
combined with whirs, beeps, and whistles
chirping among themselves in hospital creole.

Physicians' expressions confuse Spanish-only
husband, his days tending to fields at dollars a bushel
his nights pacing hallways in this foreign pasture.
He looks to get ahead, looks to hold on,
looks to build a better future for the wife and kids
through farm work and one fruit-picking at a time
much like my father's father, Don Justino Navarro,

husband, father of 10, sugar cane cutter,
apple picker, sexton did some 50 years before.

JAPANESE FETISH

Legs twitch, shoulders pinch, sweat drips down
my brow, reaching clavicle, then sternum and
I'm left wondering, is this how it's always been?
In the oppressive heat, heavy cotton garb, coarse
exterior, has it always been this difficult?
and I gain a second wind although this causes
temporary loss of mental clarity as I counter-attack
invisible opponent but I am here, now again
with more purpose

I am humbled by the real-time acknowledgment
that age is my only limitation
that I must now substitute heart for quickness
yet I cast aside this excuse
and keep punching, kicking, screaming, reaching
with tensed gaze since I know I can still do what I do

Whines and murmurs trouble me
'cause many of them don't work half as hard
don't know what real pain is
don't know antenna wire to bare skin
don't know how punched drunk feels
don't know 150 pushups before start of class
don't know throbbing to numbness to mental bliss
don't get how much more of this there should be

And I get pissed

I get pissed that they don't see
that I fractured ribs and sinus wall
that I have gnarly shins like tree branches
that I felt 50 when I was only 22
that I can't get out of bed at times
that I wanted to cry for mom
that   it's   just   too   much
that I ached since '88
but I'm still here

I can't stop loving the pure focus cuddled
beneath the surface, ready to explode at Shihan's
rhythmic time, listening to the sound of silence
between movements as we battle on, engaged
in drills designed to keep us agile and self-aware,
leaving us fatigued and desperate just the same

I can't stop because of those eyes, those smiling faces
on mischievous 6- and 8-year olds seconds after
training ends jumping, bubbling, playing tag with such
vivid laughter leaving me dumb-struck and envious
as I lay here, spent to the core
I can't breathe, trying to keep pain closely guarded
because while it hurts, it still feels good

Home

Home is sweet smell of *arroz con habichuelas,*
tostones, pollo guisado, ensalada de bacalado,
peas on the stove, simmering for those last
three minutes just before dinner's call.
It's the frantic running around, bumping into
one another in attempts to leave in a hurry,
seeking last items from mental to do lists.
Sitting silently on couches, eying televisions'
latest dramas on blanket-draped shoulders
dreaming of ice cream, home is.

Home is warped sanded wood floor
creak and crack below bare feet.
Every unexpected splinter, every indentation
familiar, yet original.
Smells of perspiration, drenched cloth, stale
air and the faint, muggy, musty smell of worn
carpet fenced within brick walls.
Grunts, snarls of pain, desire,
determination, focus, and discipline blended with
muscles kneading bone, veins, tendons
all for the sake of enlightenment.
Home is training the body to unleash the mind
in order to fulfill the seemingly impossible.
Home is *dojo*, its beliefs, ideology,

alertness to everything and nothing.

Home is a healthy fight among relatives,
idiosyncrasies that make us human.
It's frustration, anger, and resentment
brewing just below hatred.
Home is seeing another's faults not just as
criticisms, but also attributes.
It is the bonding immediately after a deep,
rage-induced cry among siblings, parents,
or combination thereof.
Home is the foundation for the root of family.

Home is the mind, creativity of imagination
through scenes of flickering eyes and swiveled
heads, speculating what is to be based on what was,
inventory of the collective individual soul.
It is the paths of figurative footsteps and
conversations in downtown centers within all of us.

Home is nervousness hesitation eagerness
angst tranquility silence laughter indignation
enormity minuteness courtesy intertwined with
rudeness, urban blight and lush countryside.
It is tornadoes and hurricanes complemented by
oppressive humidity and 20 inch snowfall.
Home is brilliant darkness, all and none,
bondaged freedom, you and me is home.

CHILL ZONE

Lines are deep, down the block
time's a-tickin' on this clock
some are high, some are drunk
but all await that dance floor funk
Aiming to chill, aiming to jerk,
to sweat and move wildly
goin' straight berserk to this beat
as they move their feet
gettin' dirty to the move as they
feel that groove in their hips
while takin' random sips
of that brew, of that drink, oh how
this bass makes them think
so freely, relaxed, less inhibited
such dope styles exhibited as they
swerve and they twirl, fellas all
peepin' that same girl
much maligned, so refined many
seek to move her wined and dined
but not now, no not now, for
this DJ must take a bow
for this bass, for that beat,
never once do they need a seat
this place soothes, that tune moves
forget the sorrows and the fears

feel that beat, wipe those tears
for tonight, we all dance
let that beat push the trance
to new dawns, to new days
look at life in positive ways
all one style, many creeds as
this music craves our needs for
community forward destiny
this love of beat so so heavenly

CONVERSATION ABCS

I picked up the phone
cuz it rang.
I said 'Hello'
cuz it was the proper thing to do.
I hung up
cuz the other end stayed silent.

UNDERGROUND

Gritty, hardened, dark, mysterious is
this current condition. Alternative detours
continuously under construction,
looking for new pathways for a better
existence. Physical and cerebral journeys
change quickly, rest stops collect thoughts
and ease tensions while serving 20 ounce
bottles from fountains of youth.
Resetting needed, clean slates sought,
white canvases desired.

Red the Tagger, as they call him, his brand
being his bookbag, searches for those same
mediums of expression. Out of job, out of
money, he can't afford them. But never
out of touch. So he creates a means to be
heard, painting underground tunnels instead.
Red explores caverns for a spark of life
hunting for a more promising future while
delivering unsolicited visions and objects of
debate to unsuspecting passengers in midnight
hours of tranquility and excitement.

Treacherous tunnels bring rush of cranial

clarity, arrival of kaleidoscopic genius,
rainbows of documents available for debate.
With multicolored palette, Red sprays his
imagination, charts his dreams, sculpts his
presence, landscaping his reality to those
who would routinely ignore him.
Here, among the rats, third rails, echoes, and
curved ceilings is his Sistine Chapel,
his Louvre, his sanctuary.

VESTS ALL DAY

taking it all in
sights
sounds
smell, typical, with metal
upon metal upon metal
colors bountiful, tryin'
to gain enjoyment from
this
another monotonous, dreary,
long ass day
in a place I'd
rather see as
go between than field office
sweat dripping from
my neck
my chest
my place I'd rather not mention
pencil nestled between head
and right ear
thinking of better times as
yet
another
stranger
requests directions

Bookstore Chronicles No. 25

I don't want to con you
or confuse you
but by fusing things randomly
confusion is likely
leading to a statistical probability
of more conning than just
sheer confusion

COOKIES

cookies remind me of milk
milk reminds me of hot chocolate and
coffee
both of which remind me of *mami*
and her gentle, always present
always available-to-lend-an-ear
love
no matter her day, her frustrations
her passions her angers
her caramel skin and soft touch
remind me of simple, delicate, simmering
dinners
followed by *café con leche* for her
and cookies and sweets for me

FLESH

I fidget. I fidget. I look around, left
and right, peering over and over my trail
to make almost absolutely certain that I
have not forgotten, I look into my power
and see what I have done, what I have
covered and I count my blessings that things
are still intact, but they can change
in fact, they should
for I ought to relieve myself of the burden of
past lies, past guilts, past shames because
it serves no purpose, that feeling,
it doesn't make me grow
it only makes me lament, rethink, fidget
and potentially feel bad for no just cause.

I fidget again for a bit in order to get
centered, calm, in the right mental space,
the proper train of thought for my next
move, whatever that may be, and
by default, I keep moving, I keep fidgeting,
wondering what could be, and I twich,
I look thankfully to the time when I grow
forward, into uncertain times and settings
only to succeed, only to rejoice, while
showing gratitude, recognizing that while I
continue to fidget, I am indeed alive

IDENTITY

I am not a performance poet.
My words don't carry that magical appeal

from witty improv, actions tender and
so poignant and silky smooth

that they simply request audience and backdrop
band to make them more succulent.

But I wish I was. I wish I had "that."
That skill, those words, that

passion dripping deliciously from vocal chords,
providing earfuls of sweet, juicy nectar while

tantalizing lips longing for a new audio taste,
another scrumptiously tuned bite

all the while captivating eyes with my
glistening gait and graceful hand gestures.

Alas, this is not me. Instead,
I am spoken word artist in print

creating landscapes formed by word

combinations on paper, I

invoke subtleties of syllables that spring to
eyes, molding panoramic portraits

engorged by pupils, acknowledging my love
of letters among straight, lined parchment.

I am a written poet, people watcher, phrase
contorter, purveyor of thought, reason,

anger, and disgust, journalist of life, showcasing
beauty of the forgotten, unobserved, unappreciated.

ISLAND PRESENT

running loads with color guard and fresh scents
daydreaming thoughts of warm rain tickling my
forearms, enticed by moist, mocha colored sand,
cooling my bare heels sipping on mixed drinks and
cervezas, away from mundane life in flashed-image
spurts, dreaming of future downtime and
living right, living light with eagerness and
excitement, adventurous spirited mind rewarded
in spouts of brilliant boisterousness
yearning for times when napping by the villa with
setting sun and subdued gaze on ocean landscape
is treasure of frequency, not snapshot of imagination

dreams of events in sun, sand, and soliloquy
with music blasts, laughter, food, and welcome are
merely a smile away, as talks of family members'
dreams amid dominoes' *capicus* draw oohs and ahhs
the distant humming and temporal beat intermingled
with tropical perfumes and vibrant island colors
of reds, greens, yellows, and blues remind me that
on this island, it's time to replenish the dryer machines

LAST ROUND

three minutes
that's it
last round
be quicker
commit
stay light on your feet
set it up
whatever you do
keep moving
worry not about mistakes
learn from them
lead, lead
fake before you throw
stay true
no mind, no emotion
know your surroundings
find your circle
enjoy this moment
timing, timing
find right distance
focus, focus
getting hit is inevitable
deal with it
train your body
grow your mind

breathe, breathe
to be a champion
work like one
do not doubt,
know
do not think,
act
do not observe,
be
do not wonder,
achieve

Nightfall

darkness looms
shadows of flickering candles
create tranquil mood
thoughts of peace intertwined with
potential greatness
want to breathe above borders
connect through disparities
enjoying soothing streetscape
rhythms and squish squish lullabies
now is time for love and nothing else
as smiling lady of distant wonder
brings images of mutual introductions
of paradise lost, nude sunbathing,
and velour bedroom pillows

PARKSIDE

words spit into imaginary mike
on an indian summer tuesday
i ponder, wonder, decipher
looking for meaning and deep
recollection, only to chuck it from
mind's window as i peer into an
improv cipher circle, gazing at
multicolored caps and hair
sweaters and bubble vests and
delicious sounds of rhyme, beat
boxes, bobbing heads and shoulders
with Ugg boots and Air Force Ones
and i think, this is live, this is life,
collection of synergy and stage,
impromptu edutainment
these words carry meaning, this
organic orchestra of free verse
provides servings of soothing syrup
and syllaballic *double entendres*
exposing emotions bigger than
bulls in china shops via gentle
banter between strangers

SIMPLE RHYME

Am not poor, am not rich
in the middle is my current niche
I dream for more, I write to see
where my blue pen may lead me
I hope it's long, I hope it's far
take me places not traveled by car
I dream in day, I dream in night
mind far away in this creative flight
I want to grow this writing craft
to show myself what wondrous raft
I have between my two brown ears
I'll write poems for years and years

INDEX OF FIRST LINES

About the Fonts

This body of this book was set in Chapparal, by Adobe type designer Carol Twombly, a font that combines the legibility of slab serif designs popularized in the 19th century with the grace of 16th-century roman book lettering. The result is a versatile, hybrid slab-serif design that, unlike "geometric" slab-serifs, has varying letter proportions that give it an accessible and friendly appearance in all weights from light to bold.

Twombly also designed Trajan Pro, used here for poem titles, derived from classical Roman statuary inscription of the first century A.D.